In the Park

Victoria Huseby

W

FRANKLIN WATTS

LONDON • SYDNEY

First published in 2005 by
Franklin Watts
96 Leonard Street
London
EC2A 4XD

Franklin Watts Australia
45–51 Huntley Street
Alexandria, NSW 2015

Editor: Rachel Tonkin
Series design: Mo Choy
Art director: Jonathan Hair
Photographer: Chris Fairclough
Literacy consultant: Gill Matthews

A CIP catalogue record for this book
is available from the British Library

ISBN: 0 7496 6084 8

Dewey classification: 790.068

Printed in China

Contents

About this book
This book helps children to learn key words in the context of when and where they are used. Each picture is described in the main text, and the words in bold are labelled on the picture along with other key words, as a starting point for discussion. The open-ended questions will also help with language development. On pages 22-23 a simple quiz encourages children to look again in detail at all the pictures in the book, and this can be used to develop referencing skills.

In the park

Parks are places that everyone shares. **People** walk around or sit on the **grass** and enjoy the sun. Some parks have a **pond** where you can feed the ducks.

pond

path

fence

Riding a bike

In some parks, you can ride your **bike** on a **path** through the **trees**. You need to wear a **helmet** to protect your head in case you fall off.

trees

path

What parts of a bike can you name?

handlebars

helmet

tyre

pedal

wheel

bike

climbing frame

swings

grass

rubber matting

seat

wall

children

On the swings

Many parks have a playground. **Children** enjoy playing on the **swings**. It's fun to see how high you can go, but it's important to be careful, too.

?

What other things can you play on in a playground?

fence

bucket

spade

In the sandpit

Some playgrounds have a **sandpit**. You can scoop up the **sand** with your hands or use a **spade**.

sandpit

sandcastle

What could you use to decorate your sandcastle?

By the pond

Often parks have a **pond** where you can feed the birds. **Geese** and **ducks** like to eat the **bread** that you throw for them.

log

pigeon

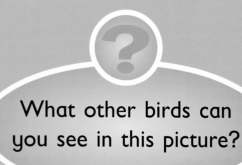

What other birds can you see in this picture?

bread

geese

coot

ducks

pond

willow tree

leaves

pond

bench

Looking around

There are lots of things to look at in the park. Different types of tree have different shaped **leaves**. Many different animals live in the park, too.

Having a picnic

If the weather is warm, it's fun to have a picnic in the park. Some parks have **picnic tables** where you can eat your food.

What do you like to eat on a picnic?

picnic bag

flask

picnic table

sandwiches

paper cup

napkin

paper plate

bushes

dog lead

dogs

18

tail

stick

Walking the dogs

Dogs enjoy going to the park, too. They like to run around and meet other dogs. In some parks dogs have to be kept on a **lead**.

What do dogs enjoy playing with?

Looking after the park

Park keepers keep the park tidy and look after the **flowers** and other plants. You can help look after the park, too, by always putting your rubbish in the bin.

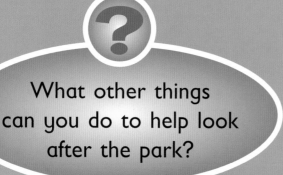

What other things can you do to help look after the park?

flowerbed

flowers

park keeper

lawn

garden fork

wheelbarrow

soil

Can you spot...?

A bench by a pond.

A climbing frame.

A dog carrying a stick.

A flask for a picnic.

The handlebars of a bike.

Making a sandcastle.

A napkin on a table.

People sitting on the grass.

Pigeons by a pond.

A fork full of soil.

The wheels of a bike.

A willow tree.

Index